DON'T FEED THE ANTS

Myra Discovers the Truth ...About ANTs

Written by Erin Bernardi

Illustrated by Patti Nelson Stoneham

July 2015

With gratitude to my mentor, Sally Burke, who greatly influenced my career as a school counselor and to all mentors who share gifts, inspiring others and keeping a spirit of generosity alive.

~ Erin

For Bill Stoneham, my herald, my guide, my love.

~ PNS

I got to wear my favorite
t-shirt and tennis shoes.
And I got to walk to
school with my
neighborhood friends,
instead of my brother Tony,
like last year.

Miss Lamb's class was the coolest 4th grade class at Kennedy Elementary School.

As a member of the Green Team, I got to collect recycling with my BFF, Rosie, every Thursday after lunch.

Yes,
all the stars
were shining brightly
in the world
of
Myra Ruiz.

(aka me)

Being a part of the "purple team" changed everything. Jewel and Marco wanted to be first and I liked to be first too. They had a lot of ideas but there was too much talking and not much listening.

When I tried to share my idea, Marco shouted, "You're not the boss!" and Jewel chimed in, "Yeah!"

Stefan didn't say a word. He just crumbled his pink pearl eraser into tiny pieces. Then Ms. Lamb used her caring voice to announce, "Purple team may stay in during recess to work on their good ideas and finish their science project plan outline."

I sank down into my seat and thought, "Being in purple team is the worst! As long as I am in purple team I won't be able to get any work done."

As these troubling ideas crept into my mind, I noticed a few red ANTs strolling throughout the garden in my brain.

Next, a new seed was planted and I felt so low I thought to myself, " If this keeps up, I'm probably going to fail 4th grade!" More red ANTs joined the others. They were wearing scarves wrapped on their heads. I watched them nibbling eagerly on the seeds of my sorry thoughts.

I felt hopeless

The next day the purple team worked on math. We divided up the work cutting out rectangular arrays for 6's. Our job was to paste them onto chart paper. I was cutting the 3 x 6 rectangle, slumped down in my seat, when Marco grabbed the array sitting right in front of me and pasted it on the chart paper.

I felt no joy on the purple team.

As I walked down the hallway toward the counselor's office, I looked at the hall pass. "ANTs"? Why does Ms. Lamb want me to talk to our counselor, Ms. Burke, about "ANTs"?

The door to Ms Burke's office was wide open so I walked in. Ms. Burke sat at her computer, her hair all silvery and her eyes framed with giraffe print reading glasses.

Her office had colorful posters like: "13 Acts of Kindness for Kids" and "Have you filled a bucket today?"

Ms. Burke smiled warmly and invited me to sit with her, asking, "How can I help you, Myra?" I handed her my hall pass. She read the word, "ANTs" with a curious tone in her voice.

Ms Burke said, "Myra, why don't you tell me about your ANTs?"

Ms. Burke was really easy to talk to. I told her about all the drama in the purple group, about everybody talking and nobody listening. I told her about too many ideas and too little team work. I told her about having to finish our project outline during recess. I told her my happy-go-lucky feeling turned to "meh", practically overnight.

Ms. Burke seemed to know exactly what I was talking about. She showed me a poster with nine ANTs on it. Some were red and some were black. She asked, "Which ANT did you see?"

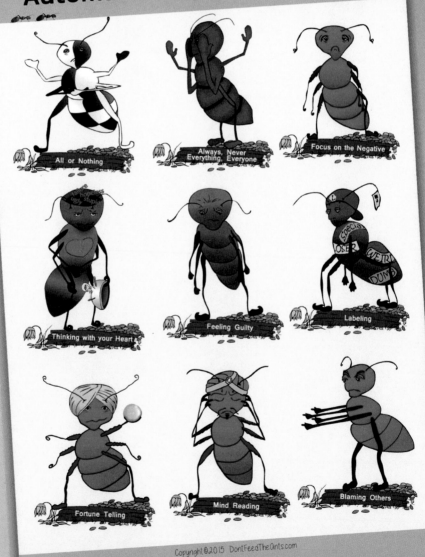

I started at the top and carefully scanned the faces of each ANT. At the end of the first row was the first red ANT.

I recognized him right away.

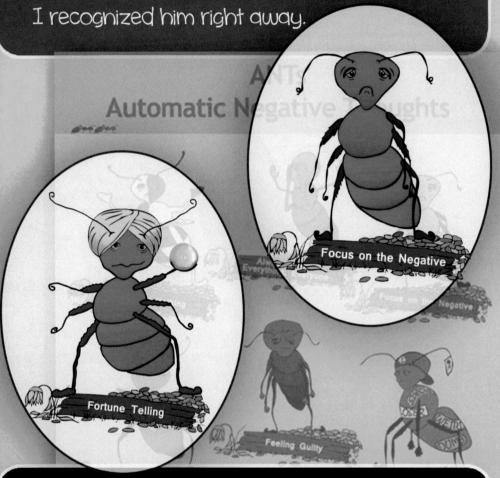

ANT:
Automatic Negative Thoughts

Focus on the Negative

Fortune Telling

Feeling Guilty

I looked at each ANT on the chart - 5 black ANTs and 4 red ANTs. The first red ANT in the last row (number 7) was wearing the turban. I looked at Ms. Burke waiting patiently and pointed to ANT #3 and ANT #7. Ms. Burke nodded her head and declared, "Now that we know what we are dealing with, let's work on a plan."

Ms. Burke pointed to ANT #3 and said, "Myra, you have told me a lot about what was going wrong in purple group, can you tell me anything that was going right?"

Good idea!
Good idea!
Good idea!
Good idea!
Good IDEA!
Good idea!

Focus on the Negative

"Well," I said, "we are studying about ocean habitats. Our job is to teach other kids about what we learned about coral reefs. Marco wanted to make a video. Jewel thought we should make a game and I thought we could use the tablet to design a "cootie catcher", with facts and pictures to help kids study for the science test.

Ms. Burke said, " Oh my, I see your problem. those are all really good ideas.

" Yes," I said.

Ms. Burke folded a paper in half and drew a brainstorm cloud at the top of each side.
The left side said, **Problem** and in the right cloud it said, **Solution**.

Under the problem side she wrote:
    1. "focus on the negative" and decorated it with a small red ANT.

Problem

1. focus on the negative

Solution

1. focus on the positive

take turns
find a fair way to pick the best idea
use parts of different team members ideas

On the solution side she wrote:
    1. "focus on the positive"

"Now that you have clarified the problem as too many good ideas, let's brainstorm possible solutions and write them down."

I wrote:
    take turns
    find a fair way to pick the best idea
    use parts of different team members ideas.

Next, Ms. Burke pointed to ANT #7 on the chart. It read, "fortune teller". Ms. Burke asked, "Myra, how long have you had these special powers to tell what will happen in the future?"

"Special powers?" I asked.

Ms. Burke replied, "You chose the fortune telling ANT, so I thought you might have a special power?"

I shook my head and mumbled, "I just felt so hopeless."

Fortune Telling

When Ms. Burke asked me why I felt hopeless, I told her it was because the team was not taking turns or using active listening.

Ms Burke smiled and said, "Myra, that is a very helpful observation and your team does not need a fortune teller to solve that problem."

On the problem side of the brainstorm paper, Ms. Burke wrote:

2. "Fortune Teller ANT" and drew a red ANT with a turban on its head.

Problem

1. focus on the negative

2. fortune teller ant

Solution

1. focus on the positive

take turns

find a fair way to pick the best idea

use parts of different team members ideas

Ms. Burke explained, "Myra, ANTs are Automatic Negative Thoughts.

Everyone gets them. One or two are no problem, especially when you can see them for what they are.

The fortune teller ANT is very powerful and it can make you believe it is real, if you let it.
So, here is some advice to help you when you first see an ANT wandering in the garden of your mind."

Ms. Burke said, "Write this down."

2. fortune teller ant

#2

Ms Burke continued,

"DON'T FEED IT"

Problem

1. focus on the negative

2. fortune teller ant

Solution

1. focus on the positive

take turns

find a fair way to pick the best idea

use parts of different team member's ideas

#2 Don't feed it!

As I finished writing, "Don't feed it!", Ms. Burke asked me, "What did your ANTs eat?"

I told her I pictured them in the garden of my mind munching negative thoughts like sadness, frustration, worry and fear.

Ms. Burke said delightedly, "correct."

Ms. Burke went on to ask a few helpful questions any kid, or any adult for that matter, can ask themselves when an ANT begins to make them feel sad or lonely or mad.

Before more ANTs make you feel miserable and hopeless, ask yourself:

Is this ANT actually true?

Am I,
Myra Ruiz,
really likely to fail 4th grade?

Answer:
No. Probably not.

How does this ANT make you feel?

Answer: Hopeless and scared.

Who would you be and how would you feel without this ANT?

Answer:

I would be Myra Ruiz, the happy-go-lucky 4th grade girl in the coolest class at Kennedy School.

Walking down the hallway, I saw my class going in to the library. Ms. Lamb stood outside the library watching me. She asked me how it went with Ms. Burke.

I showed her my brainstorm paper and told her about the ideas to out smart the ANTs.

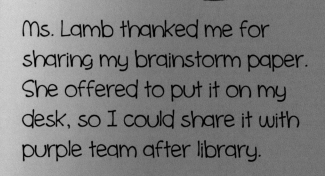

Don't Feed it

Ms. Lamb thanked me for sharing my brainstorm paper. She offered to put it on my desk, so I could share it with purple team after library.

I accepted her offer.

Well, I bet you are wondering what Marco, Jewel and Stefan thought about the ANTs and my ideas for purple team to find a fair way to take turns and get our team work done.

Purple team was already late turning in our plan sheet to teach about the coral reefs.
So, the team agreed to give my ideas a try:

1. Take turns.

2. Find a fair way to pick the best idea.

3. Use parts of each team member's ideas.

But the best part was Stefan stopped breaking pieces off his pink pearl eraser and showed the team his idea.

He took a homework calendar and in the corner of every day of the week, he wrote each team member's initials:

MR (Myra)
MS (Marco)
JR (Jewel)
SC (Stefan)

omework Calendar

MR	MS	JR	SC	MR
MS	JR	SC	MR	MS
JR	SC	MR	MS	JR
SC	MR	MS	JR	SC
MR	MS	JR	SC	MR

Stefan said that instead of wasting time arguing, each team member could be the boss on their day. Everyone liked the idea of having a day when their idea would be chosen.

So, if I learned three things in 4th grade to help me to stay a happy-go-lucky girl, they are:

1 When an ANT (Automatic Negative Thought) wanders in to the garden of your mind, DON'T FEED IT!

2 Plant feel-good seeds instead: Think about good memories, fun plans or acts of kindness.

3 If you find yourself feeding your ANTS with thoughts of sadness, fear, loneliness or frustration, ask yourself a few mindful questions:

- Is this ANT actually true?

- How does this ANT make you feel?

- Who would you be and how would you feel without this ANT?

Taking the time to care for the garden in your mind, planting seed ideas that create positive feelings, is a part of "mindfulness" and this can help you to be one happy-go-lucky kid.

The End
{of feeding ANTs}

Made in the USA
Monee, IL
01 November 2019

✈ Contents

Acknowledgments... vi

Introduction vii

1 Themes of Transition 1
Discovering What Happens When We Relocate

2 Adam and Eve—The First Travelers 9
Understanding the Hidden Losses of Transition

3 Sarah—The 'Accompanying Partner'.........................15
Moving Because of a Partner's Choice

4 Jacob—The Runner 21
Building Bridges Through Reconciliation

5 Joseph—The Unexpected Expatriate 29
Dealing with Traumatic Transitions

6 Moses—The Adult Cross-Cultural Kid 35
Using the Gifts of a Cross-Cultural Childhood

7 Children of Israel—The Complaining Pilgrims 41
Surviving Culture Shock

8 Naomi—The Weary Repatriate 49
Going Home When Things Have Changed

9 Daniel—The Cultural Bridge 55
Maintaining Unchanging Values in a Changing World

10 Jesus—The Ultimate Cross-Culturalist 61
Recognizing Our Deeper Identity

Explanatory Notes 71

Acknowledgments

Thanks to Thomas Speckhardt and the YouthCompass Board for encouraging our original vision for this study. Thanks to Bernice Speckhardt, Heather Bradley, Lari Cannon, Heather Tillery and others for their helpful suggestions used in shaping this study guide. Special thanks to the Tyndale House Foundation for helping to share the costs of the original publication.

A big, big thanks to our dear husbands, Eric Casteel and David Van Reken, for picking up extra pieces of life to free us to work on this project. And to Amy's children, Madi, Katie, and Ally, thanks for letting mom work at moments you might have preferred she play.

Thanks to Mary Horner Collins for her help in the original editing process and to Patrick Hartnett for his fine-tuning of this revised manuscript. And thanks to Nancy Congleton for her willingness to read and help get our thoughts and writing sharper as well.

We are extremely grateful to Jo Parfitt for taking this project as part of her bookshelf for global sojourners at Summertime Publishing and Springtime Books. And many thanks to Jack Scott for his patience and help in the details of publishing. We are also grateful to Graham Booth for his work in re-designing the cover and typesetting to get our work ready for press.

Above all, we thank God for not only giving us life, but also for giving us such amazing and incredible experiences in our lives. Growing up cross-culturally and later living internationally mobile lives as adults has enriched our view of God and the world beyond measure. We are grateful indeed.

Themes of Transition
Discovering What Happens When We Relocate

L ife is filled with all kinds of transition experiences. A *transition* is defined as "the act of passing from one state, stage, or place to the next," according to *Webster's Dictionary*. What *Webster's* doesn't mention is the emotional and relational toll these changes can take on us. Sometimes these experiences come naturally when we move from one stage of life to another. It may be the first time we leave our parents' home to attend university, or when we move to start a new job. We go through the ups and downs of normal transition when we migrate from singleness to marriage, from marriage to singleness, from childlessness to having a child, or from health to a chronic disease. No one escapes the changing nature of life as we move from birth to death.

However, in today's fast-paced world of globalization there is a particular type of transition experience that more and more people are going through as they *physically relocate* from one place to another. As multinational companies grow, as diplomatic staff shifts, as families seek safety, as people immigrate, as humanitarian workers go—and for countless other reasons—we are a world on the move.

1. How many times have you relocated from one place to another? Where have you lived? In general, how do you feel when facing a move?

Of course, people have been moving since the beginning of time. In fact, we see the story of the very first 'relocation transition' described in the Bible, in the book of Genesis when Adam and Eve had to leave the Garden of Eden. It continues throughout Scripture as we read of others, such as Abraham and Moses who also lived life 'on the move.' For all of them, their relocations took them from all that was familiar and 'home' to not only a new place but also to a different lifestyle and culture, where they had to learn how to operate in a new world.

And so it has been ever since. Moving from one place to another is part of life for most people in some way. In today's world, moves that also include transitioning between cultures happen with greater frequency than ever before. Even those who stay in one place for a while discover friends in the community around them are on the move. Whether we are the ones staying or the ones leaving, each transition has an impact on us. In addition, normal life-event transitions can often be intertwined with the physical moves. Children go off to university just before a career assignment takes parents to another country, or a recent marriage may take a spouse to a new geographic world. Because of all these variables, it is important for us to understand the *process of transition* and to find strategies for dealing well with the realities and life challenges it brings.

2. Which has been more difficult for you: to be the one staying, or to be the one leaving? Explain.

Stages of Transition

Though the number of moves, the distances, and the manner of transportation by which we move have all markedly changed since the end of World War II, the emotional and spiritual processes of doing transitions have not. The five stages of the transition process have been well documented by David Pollock in the book, *Third Culture Kids: Growing Up Among Worlds*. They are: (1) Involvement, (2) Leaving, (3) Transit, (4) Entry, and (5) Re-involvement.[1] To help us understand how and why the topic of transition applies in the stories we study later, we will describe each stage with a reflective question to follow.

Involvement: This is a time when we are part of the community. We know the ways of this place. We know others around us, they know us, and no one needs name tags. Here we can serve as mentors for other new arrivals to our area. We live in the present both mentally and physically.

3. Name a time when you felt you belonged to your community. What made you feel that way? What were some roles you had during that time?

Leaving: This begins for us and our community when we discover we are about to leave, or approximately the last six months of our stay, if we know ahead of time that we will be leaving. During this stage we begin to think more of the future than the present. There can be very mixed feelings, such as excitement for what is to come, as well as sadness for what we will be losing. But often this is a time when we who are leaving and those in the community around us begin to lean away from one another as we prepare for separations ahead. (This is the classic story of 'senioritis,' when an entire class of students begins to prepare for a permanent transition away from school and friends.)

4. When you find out you will be leaving, what kinds of feelings do you commonly have? Are there particular behaviors you have noticed about yourself or others during this stage? How do you prepare yourself or your family for the upcoming move?

Transit: This stage begins when we physically leave a place, but it may continue for quite a while after we arrive at the next place. It is often a time marked by a sense of chaos because life as we have known it is suddenly gone. One airplane ride and we may no longer be able to read the signs in the stores or know how to drive, if the side of the road we are to drive on switched overnight! Often the grief for the world we have left behind can hit us in big ways during this phase, despite the excitement we may still feel for what is ahead. We may wonder, *What in the world did I get myself or my family in for?*

While there may be no way to avoid this actual stage of transition and all the turmoil that often goes with it, knowing that it is normal and there is life still ahead can help us be patient and give us hope that we will soon be able to function in this new place as well. It is a time when we may need to sit down and list what we have lost, despite what we are gaining, in order to find proper closure for the past. Too often, if this reflection isn't done, we may find ourselves unconsciously expressing symptoms of grief—denial, anger, bargaining, depression—without understanding the reasons for our actions or feelings.

Sadly, this unresolved grief can be an undercurrent that stops us or our children from fully enjoying the next stage of life. This failure to deal with the normal grief of leaving life as we have known it happens for several reasons:[2]

- *Lack of awareness:* The losses we experience are often invisible to ourselves or others.

- *Lack of permission:* The very richness of our lives can make it seem we or our children are ungrateful if we express sorrow at what we have lost. Also, it is easy to rationalize away our grief if we just compare it to the 'higher good' of the reasons for this mobile lifestyle.
- *Lack of time:* Grief work takes time. In former days people took ships across the oceans, but now we fly. Life is busy in saying good-bye on one side, and, just a few short hours later, it is equally busy saying hello on the other side. There is no time left to deal with the real losses of leaving a place and people we love before we must begin to enter another world.
- *Lack of comfort:* For all the above reasons, we often offer ourselves and our families encouragement. ("Just think about how exciting the trip will be!" or "Don't forget how much you didn't want to move last time, but now you are so happy you don't want to move again. You'll do fine when we get there.") Yet, we may not stop to comfort, or validate, the losses. We worry that doing so will make it worse for ourselves or for the others who are grieving.

5. Thinking back to your last relocation, did you experience a 'lack' which made it difficult to process and grieve your losses? Please explain.

Entry: This is the time when we emotionally and mentally make the decision that, "Yes, I believe I am going to be able to live here." We decide to intentionally begin learning about the new place for the purpose of fully entering into life in this community. Finding a good mentor during this stage can be very helpful for both adults and kids—someone who can help show us the way.

During cross-cultural moves, however, the entry phase may be extended as we also go through culture shock when we arrive at our new destination. Leighton and Lisa Chin have named four common stages we often experience during this time: *fun, flight, fight, fit.* [3] At first, it's *fun* and interesting to see the new ways of doing things, but learning about a culture is child's work. Soon we begin to tire of not knowing intuitively how life works in this place and we want to take *flight*. Then, when we can't flee for whatever reason—a career, an ocean between, our sense of a call—we can begin to feel angry at this place and want to rebel or *fight* against the new order of things. In the end, as we move through the later stages of transition, we find that once more we can find a sense of belonging and *fit* into this new environment.

6. Have you had any particular mentors who have helped you or your children make the adjustment into a new place? What did they do that was most helpful?

Re-Involvement: Once more we have found our place. Others know us and what we can do. We know others and what they do. We have learned how to find the stores needed for our favorite condiment or how to get to the nearest park for a safe, quiet walk. Our name tags are off and people still call us by name. Newcomers welcome our insights and we feel at home again. It's a great place to be!

7. In what ways do you feel involved in your current situation? Are there any ways where you still feel like a bit of an outsider? Please explain.

So what does any of this have to do with the Bible study you are about to do? Amazingly, human beings who made transitions in ancient times had remarkably similar emotional responses to their moves as we have today. As we look at the stories of these 'early movers' in the Bible, you may be surprised at the nuggets of wisdom you can gain for dealing with the challenges of modern transitions. Why did they move? What did they do to make it through with strength and hope? What emotional struggles did they face? How did their kids respond? And most importantly, how did these transitions affect their faith?

We will consider all these aspects of transition so that our own life transitions can be done well. Lessons we can learn from the lives of these Bible characters can be a great help to us today. Surely the God who led them is the same God who leads us. He promises that he will never leave us nor forsake us (Hebrews 13:4) no matter how often we may be uprooted.

Making It Personal

What is the greatest challenge and/or opportunity you are facing related to where you now live? What dreams do you have? What fears? How are you dealing with both?

What do you hope to gain from this study?

[1] *Third Culture Kids: Growing Up Among Worlds (3rd ed.)*, David C. Pollock, Ruth E. Van Reken, and Michael V. Pollock (London/Boston: Nicholas Brealey/Intercultural Press, 2017), Chapter 15.
[2] Ibid., Chapter 5.
[3] Ibid., pp. 262-263.

8   Life in Motion

Adam and Eve
—The First Travelers
Understanding the Hidden Losses of Transition
Genesis 1:27-31; 2:8-17; 3:1-24; John 1:29

Certainly, it is true that the number of people around the world whose lives include significant patterns of high mobility has increased dramatically during the 21st Century. Whether we are refugees fleeing a war-torn homeland, corporate executives relocating to expand our business, immigrants seeking better opportunities, diplomats reassigned to a new posting, or part of the communities receiving these sojourners, the rapidly changing landscape of our world affects us all.

It is also true that mobility itself is nothing new. From the very first account of human existence, people have been on the move. Just because transitions have been occurring since ancient times, however, doesn't mean they were any easier in the past than they may be in the present. In fact, the original relocation transition recorded in the Bible came within the context of leaving a true paradise. It was a very big deal when Adam and Eve had to leave the only place they had known as home and enter a world about which they knew nothing. Life for them (and often for us after any given transition) would never be the same again.

While it's not hard to identify the obvious losses of Adam and Eve's transition (security, living in an idyllic world, time with God each day, etc.), we must remember they also experienced many undefined or *'hidden losses'* because of this move. Often it is these unrecognized losses that impact us the most over the long term. Learning to recognize and name these losses is an important part of doing transitions well. Let's take a look at the account of this first recorded transition experience and see what lessons we can learn for our stories too.

1. Did you grow up in various places, or did your family stay within a single community during your childhood? How were you shaped by the physical mobility or stability of your past?

Read Genesis 1:27-31; 2:8-17.

2. Describe what life was like for Adam and Eve in the Garden of Eden. What benefits and blessings did they enjoy simply by living there? Did they seem to appreciate them or take them for granted?

3. What work did God assign to Adam and Eve during this time? Why do you think God would give them jobs to do if this was paradise?

*4. Note the one restriction that God gave them. Why do you believe God didn't want them to eat from this tree (2:16-17)? What might be a reason he didn't simply remove it?

Read Genesis 3:1-24.

5. List the progression of events that happened between the serpent and Eve. What was the serpent's strategy? Where did Eve begin to be pulled into it?

6. Why do you believe Adam and Eve made the choices they did, despite the many blessings they already had (3:6)? Can you relate?

*7. As frequently happens, 'life transitions' can occur in the middle of physical relocations and profoundly affect us, even though this type of transition and its impact on us is more invisible than the external changes. What 'life transition' or internal change happened to Adam and Eve in this account (3:7; compare with Genesis 2:25)? What did they gain? What did they lose?

*8. How did they cope with the hidden loss of this life transition (3:7-8)? Was their coping mechanism a successful one?

9. What were some of the further losses they would experience, once they were relocated to their new environment (3:14-19)? What are the obvious ones? Are there some potential hidden losses that might also result from these?

*10. Why did Adam and Eve have to leave the Garden (v. 3:22-24)? Was it God's punishment or his grace?

*11. Even unwelcome moves can have gains as well as losses. In what ways did God provide for Adam and Eve during this time of sad transition (3:21)? How did his actions give hope in their darkness?

Read John 1:29.

12. I Corinthians 15: 21-22 tells us, "For since death came through a man, the resurrection of the dead comes also through a man. For as in Adam all die, so in Christ all will be made alive." How are God's actions in Genesis 3:21 a beginning picture of how he will one day correct the effects of Adam and Eve's sin for humankind?

Making It Personal

Think of a time of physical transition in your life. What were some of the obvious losses? What were some of the unexpected, invisible losses you also experienced when you left your former place, position, and relationships?

How have you tried to cope with these changes and losses? Do any of your coping strategies remind you of how Adam and Eve tried to cope with theirs? What methods have worked? What methods haven't worked? Why?

How does the story of God's interactions with Adam and Eve in their time of both obvious and hidden losses give you hope as you face transitions now and in the future?

see Explanatory Notes, Study 2

✈ Sarah
—The 'Accompanying Partner'
Moving Because of a Partner's Choice
Genesis 12:1-20; 13:5-18; 21:1–7

Co-author Amy Casteel has a friend, Jenny, who married an adult 'third culture kid' (TCK), and together they have raised three TCKs while living in several different countries. Whenever anyone shows interest or even awe at some of her previous addresses, Jenny laughs and confides, "If it had been up to me, we never would have left our original home. We'd have stayed right there. My dream had always been to raise my children as I was raised… in one place, going to the same school system from kindergarten through secondary school, keeping my same friends and family around me." While Jenny is happy with the outcome of her life, she expresses clearly that the momentum for their global life came primarily from her husband and not something she had sought, or necessarily desired, for herself.

Jenny is what some would call an 'accompanying partner,' the name frequently used to identify those who relocate primarily because of their spouse or partner's choice rather than their own. It may be to pursue the partner's career path, life calling, or simply to seek a 'better life' in a new place. Like Jenny, they are willing to go because of love, a sense of commitment, perhaps even their own sense of adventure. Surely there can be many benefits for accompanying partners. But there is no doubt that the realities of transition affect them in different and unique ways as they often give up their own plans so their partner can pursue his or hers.

The Bible gives us a clear example of an accompanying partner. Throughout Genesis we read about the exploits and faith of Abraham. But we may forget that his wife, Sarah, was also deeply affected by Abraham's choices and nomadic lifestyle. Acts 7:2 tells us that God came to Abraham while he lived in Ur of the Chaldees in southern Mesopotamia and told him to leave his country and people and go to the land God would show him. We can only imagine how Sarah felt the day Abraham came and told her they were going to leave this bustling, sophisticated city for an unknown land. Likely she went through all the stages of transition as she left the comforts of home and place and resettled in the far-off city of Haran. She and Abraham may both have presumed this would be a permanent place to live, but after Abraham's father died, God issued his next call. Sarah had to uproot once more and follow Abraham towards a still unknown final destination. This second 'leaving' is where we pick up her story.

1. What factors might make a difference in whether an accompanying partner has a primarily positive or negative experience overall? Do you believe accompanying partners can find their own sense of purpose in the journey even if it was not originally their idea to go? Please explain.

Read Genesis 12:1-9.

*2. What do you learn about God through his command and promises to Abraham (12:1-3)? What do you learn about Abraham through his response (v. 4)?

*3. How might God's promises to Abraham also have been promises to Sarah, his partner? What dream might they have inspired for Sarah (see Genesis 11:30)?

Read Genesis 12:10-20.

4. What created the first detour for the couple (12:10-13)? What new obvious or hidden losses might Sarah have experienced at this point in her journey as an accompanying partner?

*5. How did God intervene on Sarah's behalf? What do you learn about God through his actions here? (Particularly as it may relate to accompanying partners?!)

Another reality of transition is that no matter how well we plan, there are always unexpected bumps in the road that impact both the one who made the choice to go and the accompanying partner. Soon after their return from Egypt, Abraham and Lot, his nephew and business partner, experienced tremendous growth in their livestock. But arguments began between their staff over the land needed to raise the flocks properly. Sadly, while all was going well financially, the family was divided. See what happens next.

Read Genesis 13:5-18.

*6. What additional and unexpected losses might Sarah have experienced because of this new arrangement between Abraham and Lot?

*7. Why might God have reiterated his calling and promises to them at this particular time (13:14-17)?

As their journey continued in nomadic fashion, God's original promises must have faded for them. Any hope that Sarah had of becoming a mother herself if Abraham was to be the father of this great nation apparently died. About twelve years into the journey, Sarah devised a plan. She told Abraham that since God had never given her a child, he, Abraham, should have a child by her servant, Hagar. Through this early form of surrogate parenthood, Sarah planned to build a family. Ishmael was born from this union. But from the beginning, rather than creating joy for Sarah, a great jealousy rose within her towards Hagar. How often in her struggles must Sarah have wondered what God meant by his promises when they began this journey. Even after twenty-five years there was neither land on which to make a permanent home nor a baby by Sarah.

And then, Sarah saw her very unlikely dream come true!

Read Genesis 21:1–7.

8. What do we learn about God's character in these verses? In seeing Sarah's response in 21:6-7, do you think she ever doubted God's character during this long period of waiting? How is she feeling now about God?

9. In the end, we see that God worked his good plan for Sarah even while she lived her life in the role of an accompanying partner. How would you describe what Sarah might have said about the gains of leaving her comfortable life to go on this journey with Abraham and the losses she might have also known?

10. What is one main thing we learn about the character of God through this story? Can you describe a contemporary story where you have seen that same characteristic displayed? Explain briefly.

Making It Personal

Whether you are single, the person whose career path created the relocation, a refugee, immigrant or an accompanying partner, were there any dreams you had to give up during a particular transition experience? What made you decide to move anyway?

If you have lost a dream, how are you processing that sense of loss? Consider asking God to show you how he might enable you to complete those purposes, even in unexpected ways.

see Explanatory Notes, Study 3

✈ Jacob
—The Runner
Building Bridges Through Reconciliation
Genesis 27:1-45; 31:1-3, 17-21; 31:22-30, 43-55; 32:3-21 and 33:1-20

Leaving home is seldom easy. Whether it is our first or twenty-first move, each departure separates us from people we love. Usually everyone wishes each other well as they part—but not always. David Pollock often said the first step in making a good transition is the need to reconcile interpersonal conflicts before we leave.[1] If we leave with unresolved conflict, the overall transition experience can be very complicated. First, the pain and anger don't go away. Instead, we carry them deep within us, often poisoning new relationships in the next place. Bitterness can grow. Second, it can be difficult to meet these friends or family in the future. The past will come back to haunt us and we fear their reactions even years later.

Jacob was a man who knew all too well the sad and messy consequences that come with leaving relationships in conflict. He was born as the younger of twin sons into a rather dysfunctional family. When his elder brother, Esau, was desperate with hunger, Jacob prodded and bribed Esau to sell his birthright for a bowl of stew. That event led to more deception and conflict. We learn from Jacob's story that when we try to run away from such things, strife follows along. But when we deal with conflict God's way, reconciliation can become a stepping-stone to freedom.

1. Have you ever hesitated to go to a reunion or event because you didn't want to see someone due to unresolved conflict? What did you do in that situation?

Read Genesis 27:1-45.

*2. Describe the family dynamics you observe here. What character qualities did the young men reveal, even at this early stage?

*3. What was the basic source of conflict between Jacob and Esau? Of all the players in this family drama, whom do you consider to be most at fault and why?

4. Regardless of who is at fault, going through a transition without honestly reconciling differences and hurt is never good for anyone. Where did it lead Esau (27:41)? Where did it lead Jacob (27:42-45)?

As the story developed (see Genesis 28–30), so did many themes of Jacob's last encounter with Esau. When Jacob fled to his uncle Laban's home, he, the 'deceiver,' was deceived by his uncle. Jacob worked for seven years to earn the dowry for Rachel to be his wife. But Uncle Laban tricked Jacob, and instead gave him Leah, the older sister, as his bride. Jacob had to work another seven years for Rachel's dowry. Then interfamily favoritism raised its ugly head once more, setting up conflict between Jacob's two wives. Jealousy from his brothers-in-law created even more tension for Jacob. Yes, Jacob carried his unreconciled relationship 'stuff' with him. Now we read about his next major transition.

Read Genesis 31:1-3, 17-21.

5. Sometimes God can direct us even through interpersonal conflict. What were God's instructions to Jacob? His promise?

*6. As Jacob prepared to leave his father-in-law's household and land, what patterns did he repeat from the way he left his own father and land years before?

Read Genesis 31:22-30, 43-55.

7. How did Laban act differently towards Jacob's deception than Esau?

In addition to emphasizing the importance of reconciliation during the leaving stage, David Pollock added three more important 'to-do's' for making positive transitions. He used the model of a RAFT to help us remember these four principles: Reconciliation (saying sorry), Affirmation (saying thanks), Farewell (saying good-bye), and Thinking Destination (preparing for the future).

*8. With this RAFT concept in mind, how many of these important factors of transition can you find in Laban's words and actions to Jacob? In Jacob's words and actions to Laban? Did practicing any of these principles change how they ultimately parted?

Read Genesis 32:3-21 and 33:1- 20.

9. Finally the day arrived. After all the years of running, Jacob must face his brother Esau—the one from whom he stole both birthright and blessing. What was Jacob's reaction (32:6-11)? How did he prepare? Why?

10. Genesis 32:22-30 relates another life transition for Jacob. What do you believe was happening in this story initially? By the end, what changed for Jacob? What had he gained? What had he lost?

*11. When the brothers met (33:1-17), how would you compare/contrast it to when they last met or to Jacob's fears the day before? Do you believe the events of the preceding night for Jacob made a difference in their encounter? Please explain.

12. What was the ultimate outcome for Jacob (33:18-20)? What part did reconciliation play in his capacity to enter fully into this new chapter of his life?

13. What lessons—good and bad—can you learn from Jacob about building a bridge of reconciliation instead of running from conflict?

Making It Personal

Reconciliation is so important that God himself intervened to make it happen for Jacob. It matters for us as well. Take time to think through some of your experiences of leaving and relocating. Are there relationships from the past that remain unreconciled? Are there people whom you would feel embarrassed or angry to see again? If you are willing, ask God to show you some ways you might begin even now to seek an appropriate reconciliation.

If you are facing a transition right now, is there someone with whom you need to reconcile? Ask God to give you the courage to talk with that person at the right time.

Considering the last two reflections, might it be wise to ask God to forgive you for the times you have offended others, and for the ability to forgive those who have offended you? Write any commitments or responses that come to mind as you pray.

*see Explanatory Notes, Study 4

¹*Third Culture Kids: Growing Up Among Worlds (3rd ed.)*, David C. Pollock, Ruth E. Van Reken, and Michael V. Pollock (London/Boston: Nicholas Brealey/Intercultural Press, 2017), chapter 13.

✈ Joseph
—The Unexpected Expatriate
Dealing with Traumatic Transitions
Genesis 37:1-36; 39:1-23; 40:20–41:1-16, 37-49; 45:1-11

Many relocations and transitions come about by our choice. We make a decision to move after carefully weighing all the facts. Because we know this change is coming, we work hard to reconcile conflict, offer appropriate thanks, say good farewells, and prepare for life in the new place. Sometimes, though, life is unfair, and we are at the mercy of circumstances around us. Events beyond our control force us to move swiftly (for example, political instability, termination or reassignment of a job, sudden death). We don't have adequate time to prepare and can easily feel disoriented, angry, depressed, or even bitter.

If anyone knew about unexpected and traumatic transitions, it was Joseph, son of Jacob. Born into a relatively prosperous family, he enjoyed life as his father's favorite son. Joseph had it all, until life changed in totally unforeseeable ways. His story is important because it shows that while we cannot always choose our circumstances—or the transitions they force upon us—we *can* choose our response. Even when life is unfair, the grief is overwhelmingly real, and the whys and wherefores are still mysteries, there is a way to avoid bitterness and, in the end, be at peace. Joseph shows us how.

1. If you feel comfortable doing so, describe a time when a completely unpredictable event changed the course of your life. How did you feel when it happened? How did you respond or cope?

Read Genesis 37:1-11.

˚2. What part did Jacob, Joseph, and the brothers each play in creating the family dynamics recorded here? Through this snapshot picture into their lives, what do you learn about them? Do you think old family patterns might still be at work?

Read Genesis 37:12-36.

*3. Like all transitions, unexpected ones affect not only an individual, but entire families and communities on many levels. What types of unforeseen transitions did Joseph, his father, and his siblings experience on this eventful day?

4. In what ways might this particular transition affect these different people in the long term? What were obvious gains or losses for each? What were hidden gains or losses for each?

Read Genesis 39:1-23.

5. Describe the new situation in which Joseph found himself. What types of temptations did he face?

*6. Name some of the possible ways Joseph could have responded to each type of temptation he encountered. How did he choose to respond? What reasons does he give for his choice?

*7. What happened to Joseph because of these choices? How did God use these humanly unfair events to continue developing Joseph's gifts?

Even in prison, God blessed Joseph but the fact remained that he was still a slave and a prisoner. Then a ray of hope came when he met Pharaoh's imprisoned cupbearer (or butler) and baker. After interpreting their dreams and promising the butler would be restored to his former position of serving Pharaoh in the palace while the baker would be hanged, Joseph made a special request. He asked the butler to tell Pharaoh about his (Joseph's) false imprisonment and ask for his release. We pick up the story there.

Read Genesis 40:20–41:1-16, 37-49.

*8. What kind of emotions do you think Joseph experienced in the time between the events of Genesis 40:23 and 41:1?

9. Judging by Genesis 41:16 and 39, how would you describe the condition of Joseph's heart towards God, even after all these events? Does that surprise you? Why or why not?

*10. Considering what ultimately happened to Joseph (41:37-49), how might this have ended differently if Joseph had chosen to respond negatively through the years of his captivity?

As the years of famine came to Egypt and the world, Jacob sent his sons to find food in Egypt. While Joseph recognized his brothers, they no longer recognized him. After testing them and then inviting them for dinner, the time for reunion and reconciliation had come.

Read Genesis 45:1-11

11. Obviously, Joseph had been wronged by his brothers, but we do not see the bitterness they humanly deserve. What enabled Joseph to forgive them? How might these relationships have ended differently without this moment of forgiveness and reconciliation?

Making It Personal

The Bible (Romans 8:28) says, "In all things God works for the good of those who love him, who have been called according to his purpose." As we have seen with Joseph's story, our circumstances are not always good or 'fair,' but God can and will use each one in our lives for good, often beyond what we can initially see. Consider again the unexpected transition you thought about in question 1. Did it seem as unjust or hurtful to you as Joseph's experiences were to him? Did it happen simply because of life circumstances you didn't realize were coming? How did you initially respond—more from feelings or from faith? Did that change with time?

How have you understood any difficult transition in your overall life story? Can you find a potential good in it? Are there challenges or encouragement you can take from Joseph's story for your situation?

*see Explanatory Notes, Study 5

✈ Moses
—The Adult Cross-Cultural Kid
Using the Gifts of a Cross-Cultural Childhood
Acts 7:17-28; Exodus 3:1-11; 4:1-17; 5:1-9, 19-22

In today's world, there are countless ways that children grow up cross-culturally. When families decide to move globally for a career's sake, their children will become part of a particular subset of these cross-cultural kids (CCKs) called 'third culture kids' or TCKs—children who grow up outside a parents' passport country(ies) for some period of time during the first 18 years of their lives because of a parent's career or educational choice. Other children grow up moving from one country to another because their parents are immigrants or refugees. Some children spend their childhood interacting with many cultural worlds without leaving the borders of their own country. They may have parents or grandparents who immigrated and don't yet speak the local language. These children have to switch from one language to another depending on what family context they are in. Some children from minority groups may switch cultural worlds daily simply because the dominant culture at school is different from what they experience at home each night. All of these (and other experiences) form subsets of CCKs.[1] Some children may experience several of these realities at the same time. The story of Moses is an encouraging one for such families, because it is the story of how God perfectly prepared Moses to fulfill his particular call in life specifically through what he learned and how he was shaped by a cross-cultural childhood.

Moses did not grow up outside the country where his parents were then living as slaves (in Egypt), but he did grow up outside of their culture. Born to Jewish parents who refused to obey Pharaoh's order that all male Jewish babies should be killed, Moses was rescued from a basket in the Nile River by a princess in Pharaoh's palace, who adopted him as her own. Though he was raised with privilege and rank, Moses never forgot his own people, who were still slaves. When Moses tried to reenter his birth culture, he was rejected and wound up living a totally new cultural life as a shepherd in the desert for the next forty years. How could these diverse experiences ever join into any meaningful whole? Where did he belong? With which culture would he ultimately identify? Let's see what happens.

1. Consider how your childhood experiences helped to shape you. Are there any roles which you feel you live out more fully because of a childhood experience? Please explain.

Read Acts 7:17-28.

2. What were the two cultural worlds Moses interacted with during his first forty years? How did this upbringing shape him in terms of appearance, education, personality, and confidence (7:21-23)?

*3. What happened when Moses was forty? Why do you think (based on the text) Moses took these courses of action? Are there clues here about how his sense of identity is forming out of his past?

4. What was the result of his actions? (7:27-28)? How do you think Moses felt after this outcome?

Back in the Old Testament story, we find Moses in the land of Midian after he fled from Egypt. This began another forty-year period.

Read Exodus 3:1-11; 4:1-17.

*5. How would you compare and contrast the Moses we see here after forty years as a shepherd in the desert to the one described in Acts 7? What has happened to him?

*6. After God gave Moses his new assignment, what excuses did Moses give explaining why he couldn't do it? What do you think made him so reluctant?

7. How did God respond to his excuses and fear? Did that seem to help Moses? Why or why not?

Tough days were ahead for Moses. He found his brother, Aaron, and related God's assignment. Together they reported first to the leaders of Israel and did the miracles God gave as signs of God's presence. The Jewish leaders believed and all seemed to be going well (Exodus 4:27-31).

Read Exodus 5:1-9.

8. As Moses reentered the Egyptian culture what cultural awareness did he likely need from his past to go before Pharaoh? Which 'Moses persona' we have read about earlier appeared before Pharaoh?

Despite God promising to go with Moses and deliver the Israelites from slavery, things weren't going so well. Instead of the promised freedom, slave masters increased the workload and oppression of the Israelites. We pick up the dialog here.

Read Exodus 5:19-22.

9. Which 'Moses persona' showed up in this discussion? Do you think any of his feelings in v. 22 might have been a replay of how he felt after his first attempt to rescue the Israelites? Why or why not?

We know the end of the story: After a showdown and God's ten plagues, Pharaoh demanded that Moses take the Israelites away. Moses spent a third period of forty years with the tribes of Israel in the wilderness, en route to Canaan.

*10. What were both the gifts and challenges of Moses' life that prepared him perfectly for the two roles he would play: (1) confronter of one of the most powerful kings of the time, and (2) leader of a motley multitude wandering through the wilderness for those forty years?

Making It Personal

Consider your children or other CCKs you know (maybe your own story, if you are an adult CCK). What are some of the gifts God has given them (or you) through growing up cross-culturally that are useful in today's globalizing world? What are some of the challenges?

Whether you grew up as a CCK or not, take time to reflect on and write about the particular family of origin, country of birth and/or citizenship, and unique personality and talents that God has given you, in order to prepare for your future. (Consider Ephesians 2:10 for further reflection).

Have you ever felt God calling you to do a particular task, you obeyed, but it seemed to end in failure? How can Moses' story encourage you?

see Explanatory Notes, Study 6

---

[1] *Third Culture Kids: Growing Up Among Worlds (3rd ed.)*, David C. Pollock, Ruth E. Van Reken, and Michael V. Pollock (London/Boston: Nicholas Brealey/Intercultural Press, 2017), Chapter 3.

✈ Children of Israel —The Complaining Pilgrims

Surviving Culture Shock
Exodus 1:1-14; 12:31-42; 13:17–14:2; 14:10-22; 16:1-15

The children of Israel were God's chosen people. They may have lived more than three thousand years ago, but they were not that different from us in their responses to change and unknowns. As they went through the major transition from their life of slavery in the land of Egypt to living as free people in a new context, we see how they experienced all the stages of culture shock we do today.

You'll recall the four 'Fs' of culture shock from Study 1: fun, flight, fight, fit. If we're honest, we can add another 'F' common to cross-cultural transitions: *fear*. While fear may not be the overwhelming emotion, it is usually present in some capacity. It can be quite intimidating when we move from one place to another and realize we need to learn new habits for obtaining food, paying bills, or washing clothes, to name just a few. With so many unknowns, particularly the unknowns of how to operate in a strange environment or maintain a sense of safety, it's no wonder fear can be another part of culture shock.

There are also community aspects to moving—the community we leave, the one we join, and the one we take with us. Here we look specifically at the community of the children of Israel. They experienced this transition together, at the same time. The only person in the group who had lived outside of his or her culture or country before was Moses. So, as they encounter the stages of culture shock, they often respond as a group to their feelings of excitement, uncertainty, or fear. In their situation, the people were looking to each other for confirmation, security, or hope. It's not uncommon for us to rely on those closest to us when we face uncertainty. But what happens when everyone we know is also facing uncertainty?

In this lesson we will consider the ways the Children of Israel experienced culture shock together. We will also see how the God who called them to leave one place and move to another understood their fears, and provided for them every step of the way.

1. Recalling a major transition in your life, who made the journey with you? What feelings did you share as you anticipated and then moved through that transition?

Originally, the children of Israel came to Egypt by the reigning Pharaoh's invitation when Joseph was a high-ranking leader in the government. They had favor with the government then. But, over more than 400 years, things had changed. A new Pharaoh now ruled the land.

Read Exodus 1:1-14.

2. Describe their lifestyle and living conditions. How do you think they felt as individuals? As a community?

God told Moses to go before Pharaoh and request that he set the people of Israel free. Every time Pharaoh refused, God brought plagues on the nation of Egypt, each plague more terrible than the last. Finally, after the tenth plague, in which all the firstborn in the land were killed (unless they were under the covering of an unblemished lamb's blood applied to the door of their home), Pharaoh relented and let the people go. We can only imagine the joy the Israelites felt that night when the word came that they were free to leave at last.

Read Exodus 12:31-42.

3. Please explain the ways the Israelite community might have experienced the four 'Fs' of culture shock as they prepared to leave Egypt.

Read Exodus 13:17–14:2.

4. What evidence do you see of God's understanding and protection for the group at this precarious time in their journey?

*5. In what obvious and less obvious ways did God lead them?

Read Exodus 14:10-22.

6. Verse 10 describes the mood of the community as 'terrified.' When this group experienced fear, how did they treat their leader? Why do you think they reacted in this way?

*7. When the Israelites questioned Moses' leadership, who were they really questioning? Which stage of culture shock might correspond with this fear?

8. Although they could not immediately recognize it, list all the ways God was protecting them and leading them throughout this night.

The children of Israel, just like us, did not go through this cross-cultural transition in a totally linear way. Their emotions and how they responded often took several turns. After the events listed above, there was a time of great celebration and joy. Surely this was the land God had promised them, or it soon would come. But as life in their new world didn't turn out the way they had anticipated, new emotions rose.

Read Exodus 16:1-15.

*9. Jot down in the margin the word used over and over to describe the response of the Israelites. What stage of culture shock were they in? What contributed to this reaction?

10. Describe the strange new habits they had to develop to gather provisions of food. How was this different from the description of eating back 'home' in verse 3?

11. How did God address their desire for a 'little taste of home'? Why do you think he provided in this way?

12. What did you notice about the stages of culture shock the children of Israel experienced as a community? Who did they use as references to define what habits were 'normal'? Was a better source available to them?

By God's power, protection, and provision, the children of Israel finally reached the edge of the Promised Land. And forty years after their journey began, they were able to build permanent dwellings, develop their own society as free men and women, and find a place where they 'fit.' It had been a long journey—a transition process occurring over many years. In the end, with God's care, they made it. (Read Deuteronomy 1-3 if you want a quick overview and to be encouraged!)

Making It Personal

The Israelites found joy in God's initial leading, but wanted to flee from the actual itinerary and fight over the details of the process. Have you felt that way in any particular transition? Are there any people who have journeyed through transition with you? In what ways was that helpful? Were there any ways it wasn't helpful?

Eventually, the Israelite community found joy and meaning again. Do you have someone with whom can you share your fears who points you to your 'fit' rather than only grumbling together? If not, consider asking God to bring you such a friend.

Do God's interactions and provisions for the Israelites despite their grumbling and complaining encourage you in your journey too? Perhaps you would like to make a list of ways he has also provided for you in some past or current transition.

see Explanatory Notes, Study 7

✈ Naomi
—The Weary Repatriate
Going Home When Things Have Changed
Ruth 1:1-22; 2:1-3, 17–3:6; 4:7-22; Matthew 1:1-6

When we leave our country or home town and move to a faraway place for any reason, we expect things to be different. If we have enough time, we try to prepare for the move by studying the customs and culture of our soon-to-be world. While the various stages of culture shock aren't easy to go through, we know they are coming. Usually we move and settle well in our new place, all the while presuming that one day we will 'go home' when the job is over, the school year ends, the war stops, or we have traveled enough. Other times our dreams for what life will be in the new place haven't panned out and we hope going home will fix things. Even if we have permanently immigrated to a new land, we assume one day we will take our children back to see the 'homeland.' When that day of returning comes, we rarely prepare for a cross-cultural move because we presume we are going home—to how life used to be.

Naomi's story offers a close look at this particular type of transition called *repatriation*, also known as *reverse culture shock*. Naomi and her family left her country in hopes of a better life in Moab during a hard time in Judah. But things didn't turn out as she dreamed. Various life transitions occurred that complicated daily life in this new place. Additionally, these transitions made her efforts to return to Judah more difficult. When she did go back, Naomi soon discovered the difficult truth that even there, life was not as it was before. But her story also reminds us that the special challenges of reentry are not beyond God's ability to redeem.

1. What are some of the most unexpected issues you (or others you know) have faced when returning 'home' after a lengthy time away? Did you (or the others) find this transition to be less smooth than you expected it to be? Please explain.

Read Ruth 1:1-18.

*2. Verse 1 tells us that Naomi and her family originally went to Moab because of a famine. Describe Naomi's life in Moab. What three major life transitions happened during Naomi's years in Moab? How did these changes potentially complicate her life in Moab, as well as her plans for repatriation?

3. Why did Naomi decide to repatriate? What do you think she hoped for if she went 'home'?

*4. Why did Naomi want to send her daughters-in-law away (1:8-9)? What does this moving scene show us about Naomi (1:8-18)? About Ruth? About Orpah? About their overall relationships?

Read Ruth 1:19-22.

*5. Naomi arrived in her hometown of Bethlehem. What was the community's response to her? What was her response to them? Why?

*6. How would you best describe Naomi's emotional and faith journey at this point? What has happened in her time away? Whom did she blame?

7. What were not only obvious but hidden losses Naomi may have experienced at this point in her journey? What do you think Naomi needed most in these first days of repatriation? Do you think she received it? Why or why not?

If possible, take time to read the rest of the story in Ruth 2-4. Then come back for the remaining questions.

Read Ruth 2:1-3, 17–3:6.

8. Compare what we saw of Naomi when she first arrived back in Bethlehem with how she appears in this part of her story. What might have been changing for her? Why?

Read Ruth 4:7-22.

*9. What does it mean to redeem something? How had Naomi been redeemed (physically, emotionally, and spiritually) since she initially repatriated (4:14-17)? Do you think she would have dared to hope for these days of restoration when she first came back?

Looking back on Naomi's story, we see how God took the pieces of her life that seemed to be so full of sorrow and used them in amazing ways she never lived to see.

Read Matthew 1:1-6.

*10. Compare verses 5-6 with Ruth 4:21-22. What does this tell you about the significance of Naomi's life that neither she nor anyone around her could possibly have realized at that time?

Making It Personal

Have you, like Naomi, left home (or embarked in some other way) with great hopes for what the future would hold, and then returned feeling empty? What were your hopes when leaving? What were the disappointments? Have you sometimes wondered if God had abandoned you in your journey? How can Naomi's story give you hope?

Perhaps, unlike Naomi, you came home with a sense of accomplishment that you had fulfilled the dreams with which you began your journey. Perhaps you sense both: some things you were able to accomplish, others not. Oddly, these reentries can also be difficult. At times it can seem that all you accomplished and learned in that other place is now invisible to those at 'home' and something in you has changed as well. How do you also find your way back in? Reflect on the gifts and challenges of your reentries too.

No matter your particular story of reentry, how can Naomi's story bring hope to yours? Are there ways you have also seen redemption from hard places in your life, whether at reentry or other times? If you choose, take a moment and give thanks for such experiences.

*see Explanatory Notes, Study 8

✈ Daniel
—The Cultural Bridge

Maintaining Unchanging Values in a Changing World
Daniel 1:1-21; 6:1-10

Sometimes we make transitions to countries that are similar in values and cultural practices to our own. Other times we move to places where the local culture may collide markedly with what we believe and practice in our own culture. How can we relate to the new place and be respectful of the cultural habits there, while also remaining true to our own beliefs and practices arising from those beliefs? The story of Daniel offers some great clues for negotiating this complex issue.

In a forced and traumatic transition, Daniel (along with many others) was taken as a captive from his home in Jerusalem almost 1,200 km to the far-off city of Babylon. He must have felt deep longings for the world he had once known, having lost sights, sounds, and relationships of home. In addition, the privileges offered to Daniel and his friends in captivity—education, lodging, and royal food—were completely foreign to all those he had known and valued before. To defy the king's commands meant risking death. How could he maintain personal integrity, when so many of the expectations for getting along in this new world contradicted what his religious upbringing had taught him? Let's look together at how Daniel dealt with his tough situation.

1. Have you ever felt pressured to behave in a way that contradicted a deeply held value or belief, for the sake of 'getting along'? What happened? Please explain.

Read Daniel 1:1-21.

*2. Remarkably, despite his position as a slave, Daniel was surrounded by opulence. He and the other captives were offered a simple way out of the usual indignities of slavery. What did this offer include (1:3-5)? What values of the Babylonian culture can you identify as you read?

*3. How did Daniel respond (1:8)? What motivated this response?

*4. What was his attitude while explaining his decision to the person in authority? What lessons did Daniel give here, particularly with regard to diffusing potential conflict over beliefs and values?

5. What compromise did Daniel suggest (1:11-14)? What potential risks or costs were involved for Daniel in this compromise? What values of both cultures were promoted by the proposed compromise and the results of it? Please explain.

Daniel continued to speak "with wisdom and tact" (2:14) in several high-stakes situations. While he answered to a new name, wore the expected clothing, and submitted to the hierarchy of the new culture, he continued to engage in his practice of faith. After serving King Nebuchadnezzar and his son Belshazzar, Daniel distinguished himself in the service of Darius the Mede, who conquered Babylon.

Read Daniel 6:1-10.

6. Recalling the training program he went through in chapter 1, what things did Daniel have in common with the other administrators with whom he served?

7. What differences do you see between him and the others based on this passage? What was the cost of that difference?

8. Daniel had lived as an ethnic and religious minority for decades by this time. Why do you believe Daniel responded as he did?

9. What do you observe about the king and his values through this process? How do those differ from Daniel's?

10. Do you think Daniel's behavior was based on his faith in God or in the king? Explain your answer.

11. In the description of God by King Darius (6:25-27), what attributes of God did he praise? Can you see any values of Darius which may be reflected in this praise? What other attributes might he have included?

*12. What kept Daniel steady amid the cultural changes? How did others see him in the end?

Making It Personal

Take some time to consider what your own non-negotiables of faith and practice are, especially in the context of where you now live. How did you decide what are negotiable and non-negotiable values? Has living out your values ever cost you something?

Take time to honestly consider if there are times in your life when you have compromised some of your deepest values and beliefs in order to 'fit' into a new place. You might want to ask God to show you how to align your daily life with your values, even if doing so would make life less comfortable for you.

What is your biggest personal challenge or encouragement from studying these lessons from Daniel?

*see Explanatory Notes, Study 9

 Jesus
—The Ultimate Cross-Culturalist
Recognizing Our Deeper Identity
John 1:1-18; Philippians 2:1-11

The gentleman stood before us and began to tell his story. "You may see me here as one more immigrant without a job, but before the coup in my country, I was a member of the Cabinet and an owner of a prosperous business that employed 500 people." He went on to plead that before we judged others like him, we needed to try and understand the identities they had back in their own country.

Our friend reflected a common hidden loss for many who relocate cross-culturally. Whether our expatriation is by choice or forced upon us, our accomplishments and who we have been in our former place often go unrecognized in our current location. We may not have been a cabinet member, but we had an established status in the community. Now, with relocation, that is gone. When others overlook us or outright reject us, we may feel the anger rise and want to ask, "Don't you know who I am?"

We have studied how various people in the Bible handled their relocation transitions. Some of them coped well with transitions; others struggled. But there is one person who knew for sure what it felt like to lose the status or position he had in a former place; the person who made the greatest transition of all times—Jesus Christ. While it may seem almost sacrilegious to compare our stories with his, the lessons we learn from his cross-cultural transition experience can give us guidance for our own. In a world that did not understand who he was or where he came from, how could he live with such compassion rather than anger towards those around him? What made his life effective in this new environment, even though he never had a course in cross-cultural communication?

In this study, we will look at what made it possible for Jesus never to let the circumstances around him—cross-cultural and otherwise—control his responses. In that discovery, we will find new possibilities for how we can engage life fully and live with joy, no matter what culture we're in or how others see us.

1. Thinking back to past moves, have you ever felt that part of who you are or what you can do seemed to be invisible to the new community you entered? How did you respond? Were there ways you found to let others become more aware of who you are?

Read John 1:1-18.

2. List the characteristics and attributes described here of the one called 'the Word.'

3. What is the main transition John described? Would you call this primarily a physical relocation, a life transition, both, or something else?

4. What was one of the Word's main jobs before this transition occurred?

*5. Who did the Word become after this transition (v. 17)? Why did so many have a hard time recognizing his true identity? How does it seem he dealt with this rejection?

6. What type of transition is promised for those who do recognize and receive him? How is that possible?

Read Philippians 2:1-11.

7. In the first passage we read, we saw how the apostle John described Jesus. Here the writer of Philippians, Paul, tells us how Jesus viewed himself. Please make another list of these characteristics and attributes.

8. What roles did he choose to assume? How did these compare with the roles he had before this transition?

*9. What made it possible for Jesus to choose such a different way of life than he had known before? Why didn't he try to prove who he was to others rather than living the way he did?

10. Philippians verses 2:1-5 tell us how we are to live with the same mind-set as Jesus did. What does that mean? To help understand, make a list of what that means if we are to follow Jesus in this command. Are these relational patterns how we usually live?

*11. If Jesus' mind-set or attitudes towards his relationship with others flowed from his deepest sense of identity, how do we understand and define our identity in a similar way? On what do we base our definition of who we really are? Do the promises of John 1:12-13 help in this area?

12. What is the end of this story (2:9-11)? Notice that verse 9 begins with "Therefore." In other words, based on what has just been discussed, the next things will happen. Why did the mind-set Jesus took on himself result in this glorification? If you have interest and time, read Revelation 1 to see the fulfillment of what these verses are saying. It is the story of Jesus' final transition where his true identity is finally revealed for all to see and there are no questions left about who he really is.

Making It Personal

Take a moment and write down five words that you believe define who you are at your deepest essence.

Are the words you chose primarily being, doing, or role-related words?

Looking at your list again, on what would you say your core sense of identity is based?

When you are transitioning into a new culture or place, do you resent it if folks don't see who you are or ask you to do something that is 'beneath' you? If so, what clues might that give you about your basic sense of identity? How does the example of Jesus encourage you to live without demanding others give you that kind of recognition?

*see Explanatory Notes, Study 10

 Grand finale questions

Now that you've completed this entire *Life in Motion* study, what topics have been most helpful for you in your spiritual journey?

Are there decisions or practical steps you plan to make to implement any lessons learned here for future transitions? If so, take a few minutes to jot them down so you can refer to them later and see how you are doing.

If you want, pray that God will help you apply what you have learned in your life now and in the future—no matter which culture you may be in!

 # Explanatory Notes

Study 2: Adam and Eve

4. While no one can say for sure what was in God's mind, the fact is that God created us in his image, including the capacity and right to make choices for ourselves. We are not robots and we have a choice even to obey God or not. But the very knowledge of evil is troubling and affects us and God would have spared them and us from this knowledge if they had chosen to obey his commands.

7. When Adam and Eve disobeyed God, they made the transition from a sinless state to a sinful state of being. While they instantly acquired a knowledge of good and evil (see Genesis 3:22), it unexpectedly resulted in the sad condition of shame. For the first time, they became aware of their nakedness. They lost both their innocence and their sense of freedom to communicate openly with God.

8. Their first instinct was to create a cover-up for their nakedness and the shame that came with it as they saw themselves completely exposed for the first time the moment they lost their innocence. The second was to hide rather than communicate openly with God. Both coping mechanisms seemed to work initially, but leaves wither and ultimately, there is no place to hide from God.

10. Sinning can have unintended consequences. These carry hidden costs and losses beyond what we can foresee. God never wanted Adam

and Eve to know about evil, let alone experience the effects of it. Now that they did know, however, God did not want them to live forever in this fallen state which would have happened if they had also eaten of the tree of life. While we often think of their dismissal from the Garden as God's punishment, the reality is that God was protecting them so they could participate in the ultimate plan of redemption he had already planned to reverse the sad consequences of their sin.

11. Rather than withering leaves to cover their shame and nakedness, God provided a permanent covering made of animal skins. Here we see the first bloodshed recorded in the Bible. An animal was killed in order to make clothing that would last for the man and woman sent out into an alien world. An innocent animal paid the price to cover the effects of their sin. (See Matthew 26:28, John 1:29, and Ephesians 1:7, 2:13 for how this imagery is later used in relation to Jesus Christ.)

Study 3: Sarah

2. A note on the difference in names from the Scripture readings and this lesson. In later days, God changed Abram's name to *Abraham*, which means 'father of many.' He changed Sarai's name to *Sarah*, and said she would be a mother of nations. (See Genesis 17: 5 and 17:15.) For consistency in our study, we use their later names throughout. For a more complete overview of Sarah's life story, read Genesis 12–18 and Acts 7:1-5.

3. We read that Sarah was barren. In that time and culture, nothing could be worse for a woman than not to bear a child. The implication in God's promise to make Abraham a great nation likely raised hope in Sarah that somehow, someway, she might have a child one day.

5. God intervened as Sarah's protector when Abraham abdicated that role. Through God's intervention, Sarah was released back to Abraham, her husband, and also back to her God-appointed role as eventual mother of the promised son.

6. According to the custom of the day, it was likely that Abraham adopted his nephew when Lot's father, Haran, died. That meant that

even being barren, perhaps Sarah saw Lot as her adopted son. Thus, when Lot and his family moved away, Sarah potentially lost a son and the dream of passing on the promise through him if all else failed. In addition, her only female relatives also moved away. Presumably, Lot's wife and daughters had provided her with companionship and shared the burdens of running their large household. Losing those we relate to in the common tasks and friendships of life is frequently a sad by-product of transition.

7. One of the hardest moments of any transition is when the dream we pursued that led us to begin the journey seems to die. It is especially hard when we feel God gave us the dream, through his promises and guidance, in the first place. When that day comes for accompanying partners, in particular, it can bring great doubt into their lives: *Was it really worth giving up so much to help their partner follow his or her dream?* In giving Abraham and Sarah a clear restatement of the dream, God is not just reviewing the past. He is pointing them towards a future and affirming the goal.

Study 4: Jacob

2. For the complete story of Jacob and Esau's early relationship, read Genesis 25:21-34 and 27:1-46. In Hebrew, the name *Jacob* means 'he deceives.'

3. Humanly speaking, the deeper conflict between the brothers stemmed from parents showing favor for one child over another. But Genesis 25:29-34 gives further explanation about the birthright and blessing the two brothers were fighting over. By legal inheritance rights, both birthright and blessing belonged to Esau, the eldest son. The *birthright* meant he would inherit the possessions of his father Isaac. Esau, in his hungry desperation, sold all this for a pot of stew. The *blessing* included being named as the leader of the family—both in practical and in spiritual matters. He would become the Patriarch. This meant he would not only receive God's favor but also it would be his lineage through which God would honor his promises to Abraham. The son who received the blessing would become the great nation that would possess the land. This position is what Jacob stole from Esau through deception.

6. God promised to go with Jacob, but Jacob tried to sneak away from conflict once more by not communicating with Laban. Jacob sought to avoid the pain and unpredictability required in the process of reconciling. With such a focus on all that had gone wrong, he did not stop to consider those which had gone right. Leaving suddenly also prevented his children from saying a proper goodbye to the only home and family they had known.

8. Jacob and Laban not only related the hurts they had received from each other, but also affirmed the good that was there. They had the opportunity to say farewell in a ceremonial, covenantal way, and to bless each other as they looked to the future. The interesting thing is that none of this RAFT building could/would have happened without the hand of God intervening. Through a dream, God told Laban that Jacob was leaving. God knew that in order for Jacob to mature, Jacob had to stop running, come clean, and deal with these conflicts. By exposing Jacob's secret exit strategy to Laban, God also provided protection for Jacob from a potentially furious father-in-law.

11. Jacob was terrified to meet his brother Esau, who had threatened to kill him. Clearly, his deception years ago had not been forgotten by Jacob or, he feared, by his brother. During the years he was consumed by fear, Jacob lost his connection with his brother Esau as well as Esau's family and their parents. The sad reality was that Esau had also lost out on close family relationships for all these years because no one dealt with the conflict before moving on. However, we see this is another place God intervened and wrestled all night with Jacob, to make sure that the needed reconciliation between Esau and Jacob finally happened. There was no deception, no running. Jacob humbly and simply met his brother.

Study 5: Joseph

2. Joseph came from a very complicated family situation. His grandparents had played favorites with their sons which had led to broken relationships. Joseph's father, Jacob, openly declared his favorites too. After years of infertility, Rachel (Jacob's favorite of his four wives) gave birth to her firstborn, Joseph. Not much later, she died giving birth

to his brother. As the eleventh of Jacob's twelve sons, Joseph was much younger than the grown men who were his brothers.

3. We see that physical transitions can seriously alter how we are viewed by others. Consider that Joseph traded the role of favorite son for slave and his father went from having a favorite son to deep bereavement. The brothers took on new roles as betrayers and deceivers, breaking relationships among themselves and with their father.

6. Joseph could easily have become sullen, angry, or rebellious, he could have stolen from his employer, or could have taken Potiphar's wife. But he didn't. Joseph chose to remain faithful to the Lord, acting out his beliefs despite the injustice of his slavery. He believed that God's commands for living remained operative, even if he could have been justified—humanly speaking—to react differently.

7. One of Joseph's hardest moments to remain faithful could well have been this time—when his very faithfulness to God's ways led to a 'bad outcome.' We see in Joseph a steadfastness of faith in *who* God is, not just what God appears to do or not do, even when keeping that faith resulted in harder days for him.

8. Surely Joseph felt disappointment that his hope for freedom was dashed once more. His responses exemplify the truth of how we mature and grow. We read in the New Testament book of James (1:2-4) how hard times can lead to greater maturity in our lives: "Consider it pure joy, my brothers, whenever you face trials of many kinds, because you know that the testing of your faith develops perseverance. Perseverance must finish its work so that you may be mature and complete, not lacking anything." Surely the point is not to deny the difficulty, but redefine it as an opportunity for growth.

10. If Joseph had chosen to allow bitterness against his brothers to ferment and grow, he would have remained forever a prisoner within himself to their actions against him. If he had decided to take charge of his own life (since God obviously wasn't doing a good job) and get whatever he could out of it, he would have lost all the great things that God had planned for him. Through simple faith and obedience, even when nothing was humanly fair or right, he trusted that God was at work and bigger than all the circumstances around him. He made

choices to trust rather than despair, to forgive rather than to hate. Because of that, Joseph ultimately lived to see the greatness of God's plan, both for him and for his family.

Study 6: Moses

3. Acts 7:24-25 revealed that Moses had some sense early on that he was to be an instrument in God's hand for setting the Israelites free from slavery. By killing the Egyptian who was harassing an Israelite, Moses likely believed he was fulfilling his mission in life. He had been saved as an infant, adopted, trained by the royal family in the art of leadership. Moses may have felt he was meant to lead the people the way a Pharaoh would lead – from an elevated distance. Instead, he wound up as a shepherd in the wilderness for forty years—not using any of his education or princely status.

5. It is easy to imagine during these years that Moses may have felt what many adult CCKs have felt: that his life was filled with incredible experiences, but how did they all connect? Where life once seemed filled with promise, there he was in the desert, minding sheep. It seems his sense of self-confidence and any sense of identity he once had as a privileged and powerful person were gone. It is not surprising that when God reiterated the call to go back to Egypt, Moses assumed he had 'got it wrong' and was unable, at that point, to believe God could use him. He had been humbled and lost all confidence.

6. God's direction to reengage with his past may have triggered the fear that if he tried once more to help free his people, he would fail again as he did when he killed the Egyptian. Who knew what would happen then? Like us, he may have assumed that because his 'call' hadn't worked out earlier, the call itself was wrong rather than the timing.

10. For his first forty years, Moses lived in the family residence of Pharaoh. He had the finest tutors and all the perks of being a prince in the palace of the royal family but none of the pressure of being the heir. Moses likely grew up alongside the prince who became the Pharaoh he would later confront. For his next forty years, Moses herded sheep in the desert. He was in a very different place socially, economically, and spiritually than when he lived in Pharaoh's palace. The last forty

years he spent wandering in the Sinai desert, leading the children of Israel toward the Promised Land. Moses' birth as an Israelite, his time learning leadership in Pharaoh's palace, and his years as a shepherd in this very land all prepared him for this God-given assignment. All of these life experiences and cultural backgrounds joined together to make Moses capable, with God's help, of leading the children of Israel out of years of slavery and hopelessness.

Study 7: Children of Israel

5. First, the Israelites had a visible presence of God which literally guided them where and when to move or stay. Beyond that, we see that presence also marks the people and begins to shape their identity in a new direction. More than changing their place, the opportunity in every relocation to shape their identity is a key part of this particular journey. By giving the community a single visual cue, there was common reassurance, common purpose, common direction, and a common identity.

7. Going through the 'flight' stage of culture shock means wanting to return to the way things were. While they blamed the situation on Moses, they likely blamed God as the one they saw as ultimately responsible for their circumstances. We may wonder at how the Israelite community could have desired a life of slavery over the freedom they were journeying toward. But, if we're honest, we know there is often a greater sense of security staying in a broken system that we *know*—be it slavery, our family, our organization or corporation, our community— than to leave and follow God's ever-unfolding plan for us.

9. When things get tough during transition, it's easy to blame somebody— our boss, the human resource person who messed up, others in the family—rather than remembering that God is still sovereign, even when we don't like where we are. As they enter the 'fight' stage of culture shock, they are struggling with overwhelming newness. Everything is different—even the basics of life. When they looked for people to show them how this new world operated, they only found fellow pilgrims who also didn't know. At that point it would have been easy for them to feel despair and anger and believe: *If no one knows how it works here, then this place doesn't work.*

2. As we have discussed, major life transitions often happen during a physical relocation. First, Elimelech, Naomi's husband, died, leaving her a widow and a single parent in a strange land. With no suitable employment options, Naomi likely had to rely on her sons to support the family by whatever work they could find. Second, her sons married local women. That may have helped the family settle in this new land, but would they ever be willing to move back to their husbands' country? Third, the sons died and Naomi was left with two daughters-in-law, who didn't know anything about her birth culture. She was still longing to go back to her own world, but how could she leave her daughters-in-law? International living can be very complicated for many families.

4. Deuteronomy 25:5-6 cites the Old Testament directive to protect widows as well as family lines. If a man died and left his wife without a son, his brother was to marry her and raise the first son they had together as his brother's child, not his own, in order to keep the dead brother's name alive. Naomi had no more sons to take that role for her widowed daughters-in-law. For their sake, she was kind and unselfish enough to give them the option of staying to find another husband. Although Orpah chose to take that option, we see her grief in the parting, as well as Ruth's loving choice to stay.

5. In Ruth 1:20-21, Naomi explained that the name *Mara* meant 'bitter.' It was a great contrast to 'pleasant,' the meaning of *Naomi*. This was significant because people in the ancient Near East believed that their name should be an apt description of themselves.

6. Perhaps the toughest repatriation of all is when the dreams we had before leaving (and often have proclaimed to others as we left), come to nothing, and we return home in shame rather than glory. Faith can be shaken to its core when things don't happen as we planned.

9. The concept of *redemption* carries many nuances. It can include the ideas of restoration or repair. It can convey repurchasing or reclaiming something. It can also mean to clear a debt or atone for an error. Here, Boaz bought back the property as well as the wife of Naomi's son, according to the customs of the day (compare Deuteronomy 25:7-10 with Ruth 4: 5-8).

10. In ancient times, a person's lineage was very important. Here, centuries after Naomi and Ruth, the New Testament book of Matthew establishes the lineage of Jesus Christ coming from the line of David, Naomi's great-great-grandson.

Study 9: Daniel

2. The tempting offer included more than the best wine and food. If Daniel had accepted this offer, he would have had every human opportunity for advancement, for escaping the rigors of slavery, and for living a life of relative ease. But this would have been at the cost of giving up his own values of faith and practice as this wine and food did not fit the guidelines for Israelite food. By accepting these as their daily portion, the captives would symbolically be looking to their captors for provision rather than to God.

3. Daniel made a bold choice to maintain his religious beliefs despite the possible retaliation that might bring. As a Jew, this meant keeping the Ten Commandments and observing specific dietary guidelines to remain pure before God. Daniel realized that the foods and wine offered were in direct conflict with these laws and he was unwilling to 'defile himself,' even at the risk of personal loss. No matter what culture we live in, keeping our core values is a key factor in maintaining our sense of personal (as well as cultural) identity.

4. First, Daniel made a decision based firmly on knowing who he was—a person subject to the laws of God more than the laws of a human king. Second, Daniel took his stand when these two worlds collided by identifying the key issue—obedience versus disobedience to God. Third, he made his request (to not eat the food) respectfully to the person in authority over him. Daniel's trust in God allowed him to interact in quiet confidence with those of a different cultural group, rather than having to prove who he was or belligerently defend his faith. Daniel knew who the ultimate Judge was (Psalms 96:13; Micah 4:3) and did not take that role for himself.

12. Daniel's heart never belonged to Babylon. He didn't compromise his deepest held beliefs. It didn't matter what position he was in, whether

interpreting dreams (chapters 2, 4) or being forgotten (chapter 5), reading mysterious writing (chapter 5) or administering a province (chapter 6). Daniel always viewed himself first as a follower of God. His identity, his security, his home were all firmly grounded in his relationship with God. In the New Testament, Jesus reminds us in John 18:36 that his kingdom (our true home if we are believers) is not of this world. If we are a follower of Jesus, we may live in the world, but we are not *of* the world (John 17:14).

Study 10: Jesus

5. In his description of the Word, John 1 opens with a retelling of creation. God used words to create. Words are also used to communicate and understand things between one another. Both of these uses of language are reflected in the name given to Jesus here—that he is the Word of God (see also Revelation 19:13). He is the One who created the world and reveals to us who God is in a way we can understand and receive.

9. Jesus was so sure of his identity and who he was that he had nothing to prove. He could afford to serve others because his identity and sense of worth or significance wasn't based on an external value system. Because he was able to locate his identity securely, he could meet other people where they were with no threat to his identity.

11. Jesus Christ's example reminds us that when we know who we are in the deepest places of our identity—people made in the image of God who are created and shaped for his purposes (Genesis 1:27; Ephesians 2:8-10)—we also have nothing left to prove. The respect and regard we are to give others—of every culture, every social ranking, every race—is possible because our identity is not defined in comparison to them or any other external measure of human ranking, but it is one given to us by God and can never be taken away.